Metis Warrior

Preacher Timothy & Lady Alexandria

Make A Donation To Metis Warrior At PayPal

PayPal Account:

MetisWarriors@Gmail.Com

Cuthbert Grant Jr.

Cuthbert Grant Jr. was born 1793 at Fort Tremblante. He was a Metis Visionary who always put his people first. He was the son of Cuthbert Grant Sr. and Grand Nakomas Mah Je Gwoz. He was known through his life as "Captain General of all the Half-breeds" and "Warden of the Plains". He was also a fur-trader, Justice of the Peace, politician. He was the first Metis to practice and use modern medicine on his people.

He died July 15, 1854 at age 61 at St. Francois Xavier, formally Grantown from a fall from his horse.

To buy the book about Cuthbert Grant Jr go to the Amazon Website.

I authored the book under my maiden name.

Louis Riel

Louis David Riel was a Metis Politician and is known as the "Father of Confederation", founder of the province of Manitoba. He was born October 22, 1844. He led two rebellions against the government of Canada and its first Post-Confederation prime minister, John A. Macdonald.

Louis Riel fought hard to preserve Metis rights and culture, as the Metis homelands in the Northwest came under the sphere of the Canadian government. He is a true folk hero and a native rights activist. He was a member of Parliament for Provencher October 13, 1873 – January 22, 1874.

The 1st resistance led by Riel became later known as the Red River Rebellion of 1869 – 1870. The provisional government established by Riel negotiated the terms in which the modern province of Manitoba entered Canadian Confederation. After he ordered the execution of Thomas Scott, he fled to the United States.

In 1884 Riel was called by Metis leaders in Saskatchewan to articulate their grievances to the Canadian government. Instead he organized a military resistance that turned into the North-West Rebellion of 1885. It ended in his arrest and conviction for high treason. November 16, 1885 at age 41 he was hanged for treason.

Gabriel Dumont

Gabriel Dumont is most well known as a Metis military leader. He was born December 1837 at Red River. He was illiterate but could speak seven languages. His family made a living through hunting buffalo and trading with the Hudson's Bay Company. He is most well known by the Metis community for his various political and military endeavors. One of major political campaigns was the severing of a treaty between the Metis and Dakota in 1882. One year later he was elected Hunt Chief of the Saskatchewan Metis.

Dumont figured prominently in the Battle of Duck Lake, as well as the battles of Fish Creek and Batoche. Dumont's legacy is marked by his grave in Batoche. Gabriel Bridge is named after him that spans the Saskatchewan River. There are also several research institutions named after him.

Dumont was also briefly employed in the Buffalo Bill's Wild Wild West Show where he was billed as a desperado and crack shot. He also traveled and gave various public speaking engagements.

He died at the age of 68 on May 19, 1906 at Batoche as the result of heart failure.

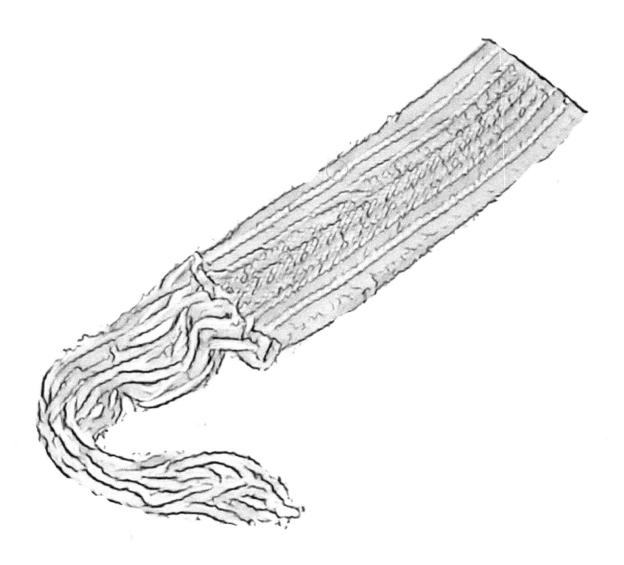

Assumption Sash

The Assumption Sash, ceinture fleche which is French for "arrowed sash" is the main type of colorful sash that is a piece of traditional French-Canadian clothing of the 19th century. There is a traditional view that the sash is a French-Canadian invention.

In historical Quebec the wool sash was used by the men to tie the jackets tight around their waist to prevent the cold from coming in. It was considered a very practical and fashionable accessory that was used by the bourgeois and habitant classes of people. The sash has a very practical use, it could help prevent back injuries or hernias amongst the fur traders back in the day.

The first record of the sash was in 1776 when Thomas Anbury, a British traveler, noted that French Canadians wore these wool belts to tie their coats together in the winter. During the American Revolution it had been well noted by Swiss and German mercenaries stationed in Canada that French Canadians wore a thick wool sash with braided fringes.

The most well recognized sashes were made in L'Assomption, a municipality North of Montreal.

The sash is a prime example of cultural syncretism, a belt made by French Canadians, but influenced by French and Indigenous finger-weaving.

The L'Assomption Sash has now become the most recognized part of Metis attire.

Hudson Bay Coat

The Hudson's Bay Point Blanket Coat was not commercially introduced until 1922, but fur traders, voyageurs and indigenous people had been using the Hudson's Bay Point Blanket for nearly 200 years.

A capote is a handmade wrap style coat made from this blanket. They date back to the mid-17th century. The HBC also sold pre-made capotes as a trade item. The HBC employed a tailor in 1706 to construct them. It is interesting to note that by the late 1700s tailors were employed by the HBC at all trade posts. Despite various variations on this coat it was the Metis style which became the most well-known, hooded, embellished with fringes at shoulders and the neck and then closed with a bright Assumption Sash.

The capotes were made from wool and came in a variety of colors. Blue was favored by Catholic Metis, white by Protestant Metis.

The HBC blanket coats that were introduced in 1922 combined the warmth and wear of the traditional capote. By the year 1929, the success of the blanket coat led the HBC to launch a full line of blanket outerwear for women, men and children. The fabric was woven In England and shipped to Canada by bolt.

The HBC coats became internationally recognized as a symbol of Canada. It was used as official parade wear for the Canadian National Winter Olympic Games throughout the 1960's.

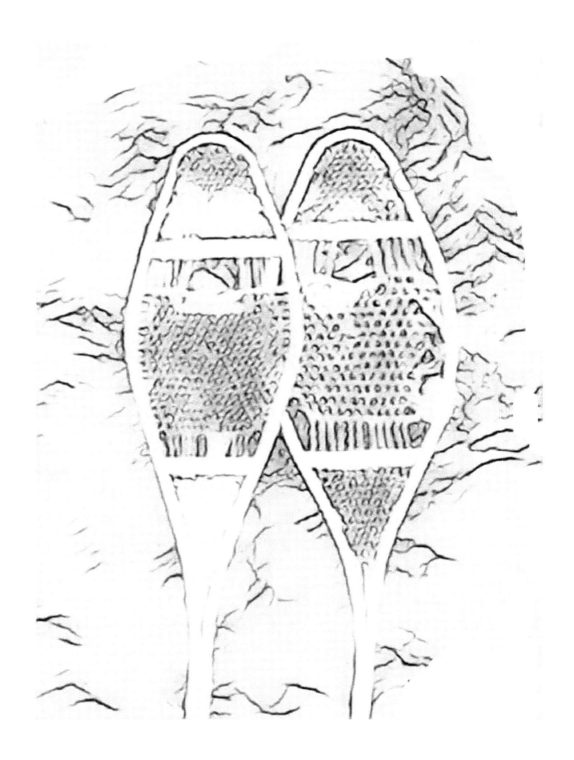

SnowShoes

When you think of the word snowshoe please consider this First Nations quote, "The white man always attempted to avoid the snow or skirt it, whereas the Indian always looked for the best way to walk on it and live in harmony with nature." The Metis felt the very same way. The prime objective was to walk comfortably on the snow, without sliding and sinking. This enabled the Metis to hunt in Winter, sometimes over long distances and enabled them to explore and discover surrounding territory. But most importantly stay alive.

The Bearpaw frame formed a large wide shape similar of a bear, they were great for walking on firmer snow through thick woodland. The Beavertail made it ideal for use on trails, rolling terrain or open woodlands.

The majority of North American Snowshoes are made from hard wood, like ash, the frame was laced with rawhide, mostly moose, deer or caribou skin.

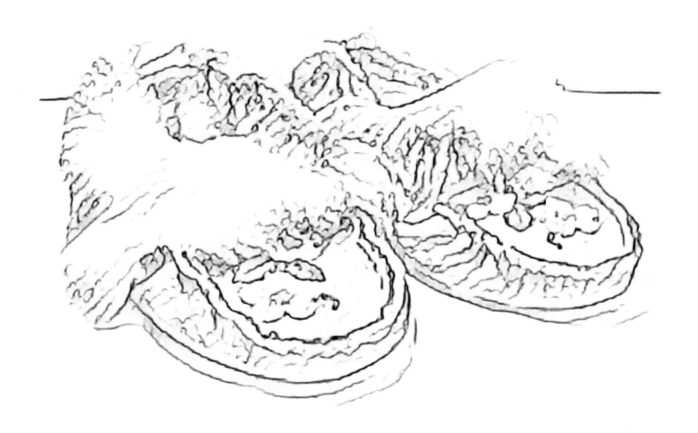

Moccasins

Our aboriginal ancestors originally designed moccasins to wear inside during the very harsh Canadian winters. Metis moccasins incorporated Metis floral beadwork. Metis women were so very inspired by a mix of expert indigenous beadwork and European folk art.

Moccasins are a sturdy slipper shaped type of shoe sewn from tanned leather. They were originally made of a soft leather, usually deerskin and stitched together with sinew. It is interesting to note that Indian people could often tell each other's tribal affiliation simply from the design of their shoes.

The word moccasin comes from the Algonquian language Powhatan, the name stuck because this tribe was said to be the first to have contact with any white settlers. It is now applied to just about any show that has an indigenous wearer design.

The Metis have kicked it up a notch or two by using their colorful floral beadwork.

Log Cabin

Log Cabin

Log Cabins were a means of housing for many Metis people. Correctly built they could keep you very warm in the harsh winters.

In the two previous pictures see if you can unbox them and add skylines and more of a yard area. This is an adult coloring book so put your drawing skills to the test. See how much detail you can add to the pictures.

Imagine if you will how you can put the Metis stamp on both cabins. Can you define the logs more? Just how much detail can you add to the already beautiful designs.

A log cabin is a small log house. Log cabins have an ancient history in Europe, and in America are often associated with first generation home building by settlers.

Straight, tall tree trunks are readily available. With suitable tools, a log cabin can be erected from scratch in days by a family. As no chemical reaction is involved, such as hardening of mortar, a log cabin can be erected in any weather or season. Many older towns have been built exclusively out of log houses, which have been decorated by board paneling and wood cuttings. Log cabins are mostly constructed without the use of nails and thus derive their stability from simple stacking, with only a few dowel joints for reinforcement. This is because a log cabin tends to compress slightly as it settles, over a few months or years. Nails would soon be out of alignment and torn out.

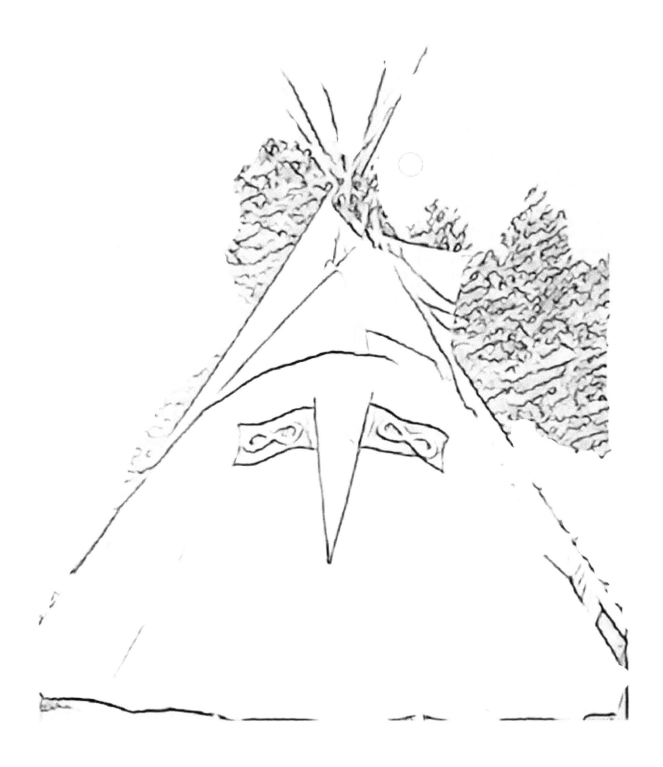

Teepee

A teepee, also known as tipi is in its simple terms a cone shaped tent, in the traditional sense it is made from animal hides that are upon animal hides. You can tell the difference from conical tents by the smoke flaps at the very top of it. These were used by indigenous people of the Plains and the Canadian Prairies of North America.

They were durable, provided warmth in the Winter and stayed cool in the heat of the summer. They can be disassembled and packed away quickly when the people needed to relocate. This portability was important to Plains Indians and their nomadic lifestyles.

The word tipi comes from the Lakota language, means "a dwelling" od "they dwell". As a lot of Metis were buffalo hunters and had indigenous wives and family trees, they would have used these as it allowed them to follow game migrations such as bison.

They are now primarily used today for ceremonial purposes.

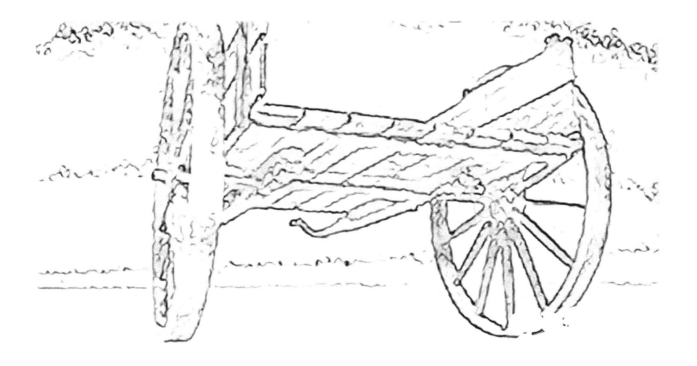

Metis Cart

Metis Cart

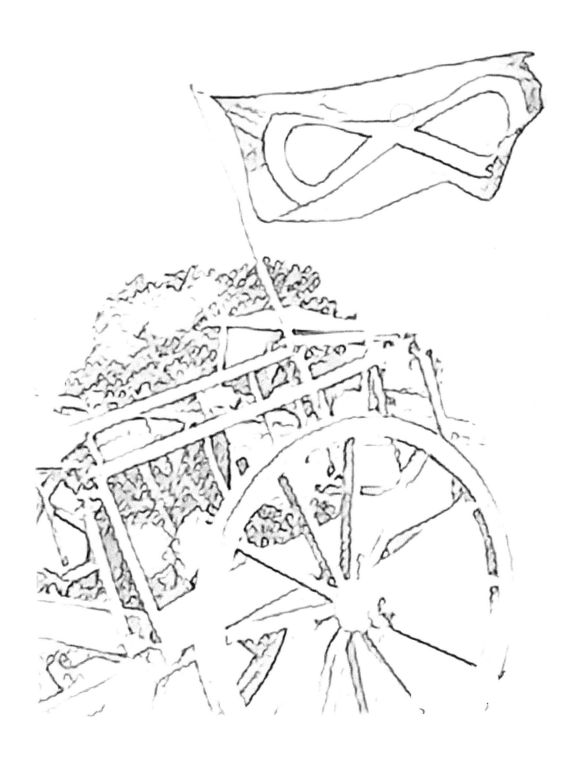

Metis Cart

The Metis Cart was first used by Metis to bring meat from the buffalo hunt and later used as well in farm work. It is a very large two-wheeled cart made entirely out of non- metal parts. It was often pulled by oxen and horses and mules were also used. They were in use throughout most of the 19th century in the fur-trade and the westward expansion in Canada.

With these carts the Metis were not restricted to river travel only in order to hunt bison. It has been said the Metis cart was largely responsible for commercializing the buffalo hunt.

The Metis cart was developed Metis and Anglo-Metis peoples and it is sometimes used today as a symbol of Metis nationalism.

Because nails were not available or that they were very expensive, in the early West, the carts contained no iron at all, they were constructed entirely of wood and animal hide. The carts could be dismantled, and the wheels covered with bison hides to make floats and the box placed at the top. Thus, the cart could be floated across streams.

Some carts were strong enough to carry loads as heavy as 1,000 pounds.

Horse

Horse Pulling Cart

Metis people had a very special relationship with their horses. Riders even performed acrobatic feats on horseback and held competitions. They would pick up an object up off the ground while riding at full gallop. They were adept with the lasso, using the term "cabresser", for throwing the rope.

Metis horses were proudly adorned with fancy quill and beadwork decorations. Horses helped Metis earn a living by being an essential part of the buffalo hunt. A rider had to trust their horse's obedience, speed and stamina, qualities that could mean the difference between life and death during the bison hunt.

Horses allowed Metis to do:

- Travel great distances
- Hunt buffalo in wider area
- Kill more buffalo – chase and shoot
- Use Metis carts

Bison

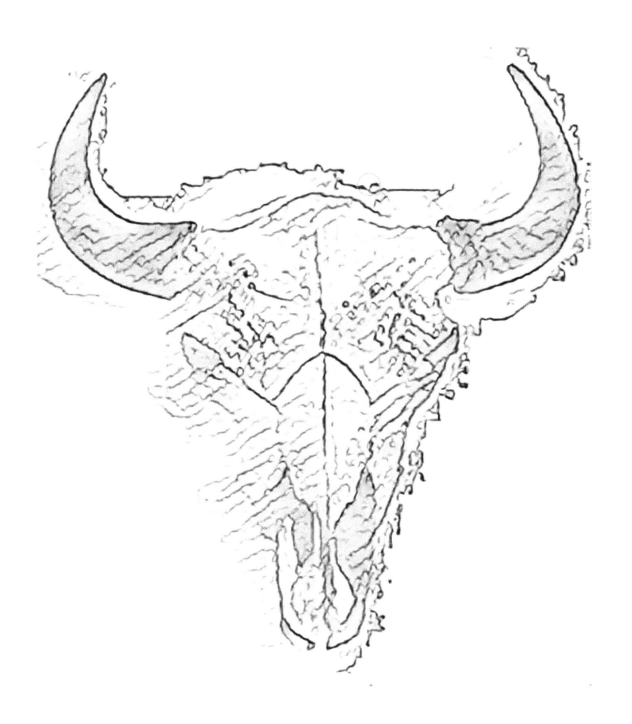

Bison Skull

Bison was an important part of any Metis life. The Bison not only provided food but also provided clothing, weapons, and tools. The food came from the meat of the Bison and the Clothing from the hide. Weapons and Tools were made from the bones, teeth, and horns.

Not only could the Bison hide provide clothing, but it also provided shelter, and covering for the carts.

Use your imagination in the picture and add to the Bison's environment. Let's see what you can add to the picture.

Bison meat is sold in many stores still today. The Metis people valued every part of the Bison and wasted nothing. They found a use for every part from the Bison.

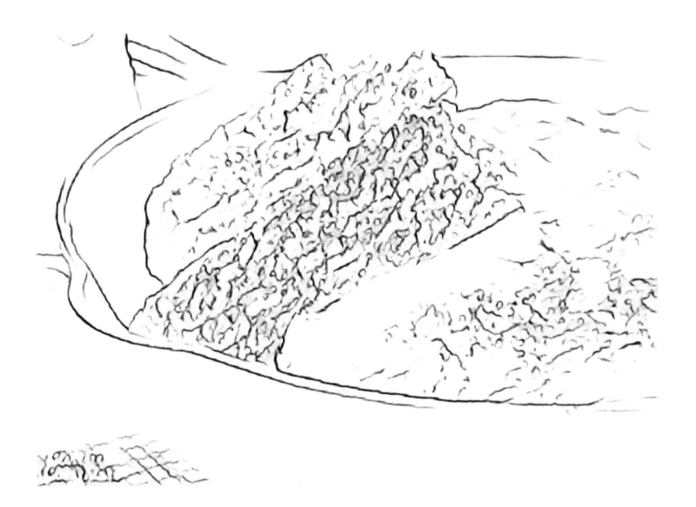

Bannock

Bannock On A Stick

Bannock is a flat quick bread. The word bannock comes from Northern and Scots dialects. It has been said the term comes from panicium, a Latin word for "baked Dough", or from panis, meaning bread. Its historic use was primarily in Ireland, Scotland and Northern England.

The original bannock was very heavy, and barley and oatmeal dough were used. Most modern bannock is made with baking powder or baking soda. There has been a train of thought that bannock played a key role in deciding if a person was to be used as a human sacrifice during the late Iron Age in the discovery of Lindow Man.

Metis bannock is also known as Indian Bread and can be fried or baked in the oven. It is great with soup and served with butter and jam.

The bannock that originated in Scotland was eventually adopted by the Metis people. The Gaelic word bannach, means "morsel".

Bannock can also be wrapped around a stick and cooked over an open fire. It is a source of carbs and a fulfilling meal, which was a staple for wilderness explorers, trappers and prospectors.

Pemmican

Pemmican is a highly concentrated mixture of fat and protein used as a nutritious food. It was invented by the indigenous peoples of North America. The word comes from the Cree word pimihkan, which itself is derived from the word pimi, "fat grease".

The ingredients used were usually whatever was available., The meat was often bison, deer, elk or moose. Fruits such as cranberries and saskatoon berries.

Whatever meat that was used was cut into thin slices and dried, either by slow fire or in the hot sun until it was hard and brittle. It was then pounded into small pieces, almost powder-like. The pounded meat was mixed with melted fat and in some cases dried fruit was pounded into powder and added to meat/fat mixture. The end result was then packed into rawhide bags for storage. At room temperature pemmican can generally last one to five years.

A bag of bison pemmican weighing about 90 lb was called taureau (French for bull) by the Metis.

This is an ideal food for hunts and travelling between various fur trade posts.

Fiddle

Metis fiddle is a very unique style in which the Metis of Canada and the Northern United States have made their own in which to play the violin. Both as solo and folk ensembles. Fiddles were introduced to the Metis by Scottish and French – Canadian fur traders in the early 1800's.

Music was a very important part of Metis culture and heritage. They played jigs, reels and various dances.

Metis fiddle tradition is an aural tradition which cannot be taught in schools. Metis fiddle players are known for using their feet and choke up on the bow to enable a very sharp bite.

Red River Jig

Red River Jig

The Red River Jig is known as the traditional dance of the Metis people. The origins of the dance lie in the traditional dances of the First Nations, French, English, Scots and Orcadian peoples from where the Metis people have come from. The name refers to the Red River in the North which forms a border between North Dakota and Minnesota.

"Jigging", as it is most commonly referred to by Metis people is very similar to the traditional dances of Quebec and Canadian Maritime communities of British Isles heritage. It has also been called by some as the Metis national anthem.

Sage

Sweet Grass

Sage is used by Indigenous peoples and Metis of North America. It is used in the smudging ceremony that involves the burning of sage for spiritual cleansing and or blessings. Smudging can be used to combat negativity and clear your energy field. The goal of smudging is to make your home or your environment clear of lingering energy, make it a positive place. We are welcoming the Great Spirit, angels, and ancestors to come and share clean space. Smudging can also produce visions, it can also be used to purify tools before an important spiritual ceremony.

Many Elders have said that the Spirits like the aroma produced when we burn sacred herbs like sage and sweet grass.

Sweet grass can be used to bring ease to a space when we need to discuss a difficult situation. This plant is the sacred hair of Mother Earth, its sweet aroma reminds people of the gentleness, love and kindness she has for the people, this is why Indigenous people pick it and braid it in 3 stands representing love, kindness and honesty. It can also be used like sage for smudging and purification of the spirit. It has a calming effect.

METIS WARRIOR

By This Point You Should Know Who These 3 Are

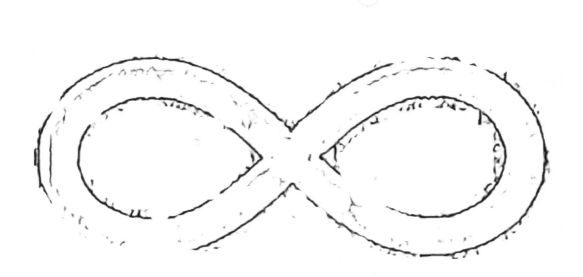

Metis Flag

The Metis flag belongs to all Metis People. It was first used by Metis resistance fighters in Canada before 1816. It had been received as a gift from Alexander MacDonell of Greenfield of the North West Company in 1814. The Metis flag shows an infinity symbol on a filed of either blue or red. The white infinity symbol represents the faith that the Metis culture will live forever. It is also perceived as the joining or unity of two cultures, Aboriginal First Nations and European.

Cuthbert Grant Jr. flew this flag into battle at the Battle of Seven Oaks, 1816. It is considered the oldest Canadian patriotic flag indigenous to Canada.

The Metis flag is similar to that of the national flag of Scotland which features a white x on a blue background and that of French Canada, which features the white fleur di lis on a very similar blue background.

Dream Catcher

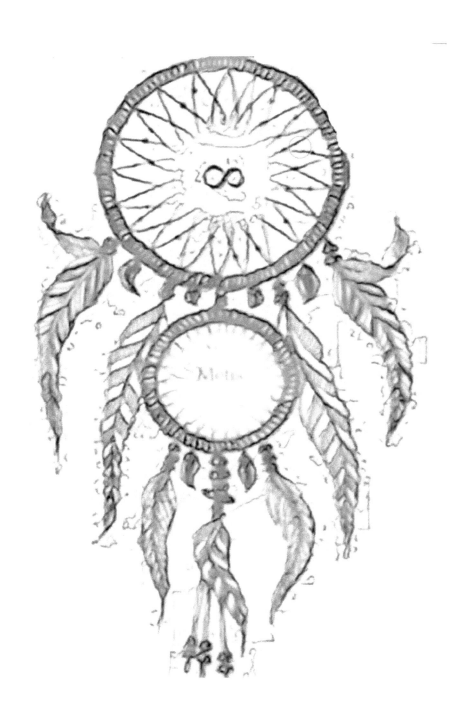

Dream Catcher

A Dream Catcher is a sacred Native American object that are used to encourage good dreams. Ojibwe and Lakota lore depict them as either trapping good and bad dreams, but the feathers are always to direct the good dreams to the owner of the dream catcher.

They are made from a ring of red willow or any other similarly common pliable bark. It is held together by a web of sinew or fiber that connects to the ring in seven or eight places.

There are many legends that surround the dream catchers and they seem to revolve around similar themes, spirits and spiders. Dream catchers were made by grandmothers of newborn infants and hung above their cradle boards.

As dream catchers are made from organic materials, they are designed to disintegrate over time as the child grows into an adult.

Crest of Siol Cudbright

A Sept is much like a subdivision of a Clan. A clan is analogous to a large, extended family and came into being for many reasons. It could have been due to divisions, sometimes violent, or it could have been a restless son wishing to settle elsewhere with the full blessing and support of the Clan and its Chief.

Siol Cudbright is the Official Sept of Clan Grant in Scotland. They are the Metis descendants of Cuthbert Grant Sr. of Cromdale, Scotland. This Sept was officially formed when Lord Strathspey, The Rt. Hon Sir James Grant of Grant, The 6th Lord Strathspey, Baronet of Nova Scotia, 33rd Chief of Clan Grant came to Winnipeg, Manitoba Canada in 2012 and made Sandra (Alexandria Horyski) Anthony the first Sept Stewart.

This is the Official logo and crest of Siol Cudbright.

Other Books By Lady Alexandria

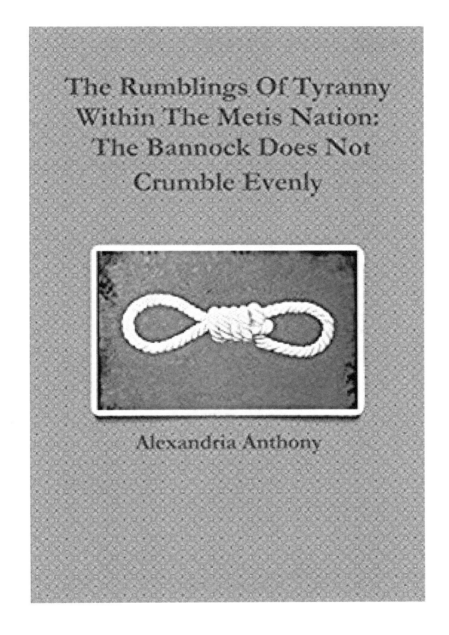

The Rumblings Of Tyranny
Within The Metis Nation:
The Bannock Does Not
Crumble Evenly

Alexandria Anthony

ALEXANDRIA ANTHONY

What Being Metis Means To Me

Exorcising Shame and
Hiding in Plain Sight

Other Books By Preacher Timothy

VLAD III

"The Impaler"

Timothy Mark

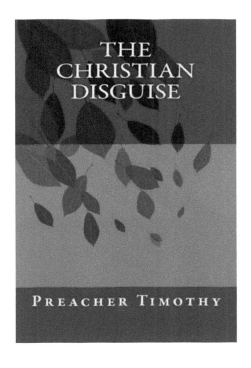

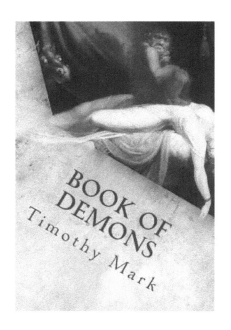

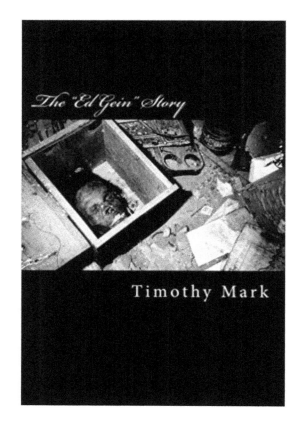

We at Metis Warrior hope you enjoyed this educational coloring book. Please take the next few pages to draw your representation of Metis Pride.

We have included 5 pages so the family can draw their own version of Metis Pride. We are taking donations on our website as well as at PayPal.

Our WebSite: MetisWarrior.Com

Our PayPal Account: MetisWarriors@Gmail.Com

Adult Metis Coloring Book

Until Next Time

9 780359 382439